THE *Little Book* OF

~

LOVE

~

**A TREASURY OF
THE MANY FACETS
OF LOVE**

Editor: Fleur Robertson
Editorial Assistance: Nicola Dent, Laura Potts, Jillian Stewart
Text Contributors: Louise Houghton, Fleur Robertson
Original Design Concept: Peter Bridgewater, Nigel Duffield
Design: Jill Coote
Picture Research: Leora Kahn
Director of Production: Gerald Hughes
Typesetting: Julie Smith

MALLARD PRESS
An imprint of BDD Promotional Book Company, Inc.,
666 Fifth Avenue, New York, NY 10103.
Mallard Press and its accompanying duck logo
are trademarks of BDD Promotional Book Company, Inc.,
registered in the U.S. Patent and Trademark Office. Copyright © 1992.

CLB 3145
© 1992 Colour Library Books Ltd, Godalming, Surrey, England.
First published in the United States of America in 1992 by The Mallard Press.
Printed and bound in Singapore.

ISBN 0-7924-5813-3

THE *Little Book* OF

LOVE

MALLARD
PRESS

$\mathcal{I}ntroduction$

Love, once experienced in all its perfection, is rarely forgotten. Indeed, sometimes a great love, or the memory of it, will last a lifetime. The poetry and prose on the following pages was written by men and women who knew love and their words are proof of this. From the passionate, impatient language of the letter Napoleon Bonaparte sent to his beloved Josephine, to the heartfelt words penned by a soldier to his wife during the First World War, these pages reflect the many varied ways people have responded to this powerful emotion. Here is a much-loved fairytale from *The Thousand and One Nights*; the true story of an Indian king's adoration; a patriot's belief; and the delight of a mother in her child. Here too are some of the most romantic sonnets ever written. With each page beautifully illustrated, this exquisite volume will serve as the perfect reminder for anyone who has known love.

A Wife's Love

If ever two were one, then surely we.
If ever man were loved by wife, then thee;
If ever wife was happy in a man,
Compare with me, ye women, if you can.
I prize thy love more than whole mines of gold
Or all the riches that the East doth hold.
My love is such that rivers cannot quench,
Nor aught but love from thee give recompense.
Thy love is such I can no way repay;
The heavens reward thee manifold, I pray.
Then while we live, in love let's so persevere,
Then when we live no more we may live ever.

TO MY DEAR AND LOVING HUSBAND
Anne Bradstreet

A Valentine

O, once I had a true love,
As blest as I could be:
Patty was my turtle dove,
And Patty she loved me.
We walked the fields together,
By roses and woodbine,
In summer's sunshine weather,
And Patty, she was mine.

Then Patty was a slight young thing;
Now she's long past her teens;
And we've been married many springs,
And mixed in many scenes.
And I'll be true for Patty's sake,
And she'll be true for mine;
And I this little ballad make,
To be her Valentine.

A VALENTINE TO MY WIFE
John Clare

I am
thine
Love.

Oh be
thou
mine.

Love in Later Life

Your wedding ring wears thin, dear wife;
    ah, summers not a few
Since I put it on your finger first
    have passed o'er me and you;
And, love, what changes we have seen
    – what cares and pleasures too –
Since you became my own dear wife,
    when this old ring was new!

The past is dear, its sweetness still
    our memories to reassure yet.
The griefs we've borne, together borne,
    we would not now forget.
Whatever, wife, the future brings,
    heart unto heart still true,
We'll share as we have shared all else
    since this old ring was new.

THE WORN WEDDING RING
Anon

A Love Sonnet

How do I love thee? Let me count the ways.
    I love thee to the depth and breadth and height
My soul can reach, when feeling out of sight
    For the end of Being and ideal Grace.
I love thee to the level of every day's
    Most quiet need, by sun and candle-light.
I love thee freely, as men strive for Right;
    I love thee purely, as men turn from Praise.
I love thee with the passion put to use
    In my old griefs, and with my childhood's faith.
I love thee with a love I seemed to lose
    With my lost saints, – I love thee with the breath,
        Smiles, tears, of all my life! – and, if God choose,
        I shall but love thee better after death.

A SONNET FROM THE PORTUGUESE
Elizabeth Barrett-Browning

First Love

....

Juliet ... Dost thou love me? I know thou wilt say aye;
And I will take thy word: yet, if thou swear'st,
Thou may prove false; at lovers' perjuries
They say Jove laughs. O gentle Romeo,
If thou dost love, pronounce it faithfully:
Or, if thou think'st I am too quickly won,
I'll frown, and be perverse, and say thee nay,
So thou wilt woo; but else, not for the world.
In truth, fair Montague, I am too fond;
And therefore thou mayst think my 'haviour light:
But trust me, gentleman, I'll prove more true
Than those that have more cunning to be strange....

ROMEO AND JULIET, ACT 2, SCENE 1
William Shakespeare

A Soldier's Love

My darling Lizzie,

At last I have the opportunity of writing to you a real letter. In the first place, dearest, I trust you and the children are quite well. I guess you have been worried with the air raids. You know, dear, it's hard to be out here fighting, and yet your wife and children can't be safe.... We are expecting to go up again in 2 or 3 days, so dearest, pray hard for me and ask Marie for God will not refuse her prayers. She doesn't know the wickedness of this world. Dear Lizzie, it's nearly six months now since I saw you all. I love you more than ever. I long to take you in my arms again, what a lot of love we have missed but please God, it will make it all the sweeter when I see you. I often take your photo out of my pocket and look at your dear face and think of the times we have had together, some lovely days, oh love, and when I think again of some of the worry I have caused you, it makes me only the more eager to get home to you to atone for all the worry and anxious moments you have had to put up with. You always stuck by me in all things, dear God bless you for it....Please God it won't be long before this war is over. We are pushing old Fritz back and I don't think he will stand the British boys much longer and then we will try and keep a nice home. I will know the value of one now.... Goodnight love, God bless you and my children and may He soon send me back to those I love is the wish of your Faithful Husband,

Jack

Private John Mudd died in action in 1917, four days after writing this letter.

An Emperor's Love

I wake filled with thoughts of you. Your portrait and the intoxicating evening which we spent yesterday have left my senses in turmoil. Sweet, incomparable Josephine, what a strange effect you have on my heart! Are you angry? Do I see you looking sad? Are you worried?... My soul aches with sorrow, and there can be no rest for your lover; but there is still more in store for me when, yielding to the profound feelings which overwhelm me, I draw from your lips, from your heart a love which consumes me with fire? Ah! it was last night that I fully realised how false an image of you your portrait gives!

You are leaving at noon; I shall see you in three hours.

Until then, *mio dolce amor*, a thousand kisses; but give me none in return, for they set my blood on fire.

LETTER TO JOSEPHINE, PARIS, DECEMBER 1795
Napoleon Bonaparte

Eternal Love

Shall I compare thee to a summer's day?
 Thou art more lovely and more temperate:
Rough winds do shake the darling buds of May,
 And summer's lease hath all too short a date:
Sometime too hot the eye of heaven shines,
 And often is his gold complexion dimmed;
And every fair from fair sometime declines,
 By chance, or nature's changing course untrimmed;
But thy eternal summer shall not fade,
 Nor lose possession of that fair thou owest,
Nor shall death brag thou wanderest in his shade,
 When in eternal lines to time thou growest;
  So long as men can breathe, or eyes can see,
  So long lives this, and this gives life to thee.

SONNET XVIII
William Shakespeare

Infant Love

When thou first camest, gentle, shy and fond,
  My eldest born, first hope, and dearest treasure,
My heart received thee with a joy beyond
  All that it yet had felt of earthly pleasure;
    Nor thought that any love again might be
    So deep and strong as that I felt for thee.

THE MOTHER'S HEART (1ST VERSE)
Caroline E. Norton

26

A Love Potion

Combined with the warmth of spirits such as Armagnac and Madeira, this Renaissance drink, *Sabayon*, is an effective love potion when served hot or cold. Raw egg yolks are full of protein and minerals – energy-giving foods beloved as aphrodisiacs by both the French and the Arabs – while honey is known for its invigorating qualities the world over. The French, it should be noted, take this potion while it is still hot.

Ingredients
Three raw egg yolks
Three tablespoons of honey
Three tablespoons of Madeira
One tablespoon of Armagnac
One dessertspoon of brown sugar

Method
Mix the ingredients in a bowl over a pan of hot water and beat until frothy. Drink straight away, and await the inspiring effects to come....

Forbidden Love

'Twas a new feeling – something more
Than we had dared to own before,
  Which then we hid not;
We saw it in each other's eye,
And wished, in every half-breathed sigh,
  To speak, but did not.

She felt my lips' impassioned touch –
'Twas the first time I dared so much,
  And yet she chid not;
But whispered o'er my burning brow,
'Oh, do you doubt I love you now?'
  Sweet soul! I did not.

Warmly I felt her bosom thrill,
I pressed it closer, closer still,
  Though gently bid not;
Till – oh! the world had seldom heard
Of lovers, who so nearly erred,
  And yet, who did not.

Thomas Moore

A Scotsman's Love

O my Luve's like a red, red rose
That's newly sprung in June:
O my Luve is like the melody
That's sweetly play'd in tune. –

As fair art thou, my bonnie lass,
So deep in luve am I:
And I will luve thee still, my dear,
Till a' the seas gang dry. –

Till a' the sea gang dry, my Dear,
And the rocks melt wi' the sun:
And I will luve thee still, my dear,
While the sands o' life shall run. –

And fare thee weel, my only Luve!
And fare thee weel a while!
And I will come again, my Luve,
Tho' it were ten thousand mile.

A RED, RED ROSE
Robert Burns

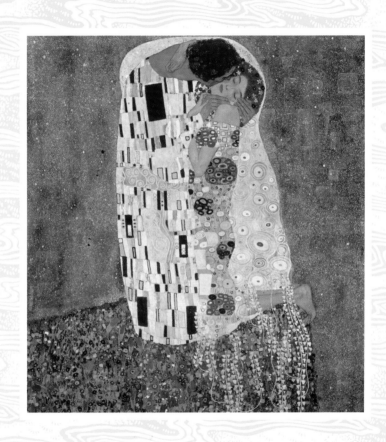

A Poet's Love

Had I the heavens' embroidered cloths,
Enwrought with golden and silver light,
The blue and the dim and the dark cloths
Of night and light and the half-light,
I would spread the cloths under your feet:
But I, being poor, have only my dreams;
I have spread my dreams under your feet;
Tread softly because you tread on my dreams.

HE WISHES FOR THE CLOTHS OF HEAVEN
W. B. Yeats

Married Love

Dearly beloved: We are gathered here today in the eyes of the Lord and the sight of this congregation to join this man and this woman in Holy Matrimony. The bond and covenant of marriage was established by God in creation, and our Lord Jesus Christ adorned this manner of life by his presence and first miracle at a wedding in Cana of Galilee. It signifies to us the mystery of the union between Christ and his Church, and the Holy Scripture commends it to be honored among all people.

The union of husband and wife in heart, body and mind is intended by God for their mutual joy; for the help and comfort given one another in prosperity and adversity; and, when it is God's will, for the procreation of children and their nurture in the knowledge and love of the Lord. Therefore marriage is not to be entered into unadvisedly or lightly, but reverently, deliberately, and in accordance with the purposes for which it was instituted by God.

THE MARRIAGE SERVICE
The Book of Common Prayer

Love of Home

From the gay world we'll oft retire
   To our own family and fire,
      Where love our hours employs
No noisy neighbour enters here,
   No intermeddling stranger near,
      To spoil our heartfelt joys.

If solid happiness we prize,
   Within our breasts this jewel lies,
      And they are fools that roam;
The world hath nothing to bestow, –
   From our own selves our bliss must flow,
      And that dear hut, our home.

THE FIRESIDE
Anon

Biblical Love

As an apple tree among the trees of the wood,
    so is my beloved among young men.
I delighted and sat down under his shadow,
    and his fruit was sweet to my taste.
He brought me to the house of wine,
    and his banner over me was love.
Stay me with flagons, comfort me with apples:
    for I am sick with love.
O that his left hand were under my head,
    And that his right hand embraced me!

CHAPTER 2, VERSES 3-6
The Song of Solomon

The Lightest Love

Fair Iris I love, and hourly I die,
  But not for a lip nor a languishing eye:
She's fickle and false, and there we agree,
  But I am as false and as fickle as she;
    We neither believe what either can say,
    And, neither believing, we neither betray.

'Tis civil to swear and say things, of course;
  We mean not the taking for better for worse;
When present, we love; when absent, agree:
  I think not of Iris, nor Iris of me.
    The legend of love no couple can find
    So easy to part, or so equally joined.

MERCURY'S SONG
John Dryden

The Chosen

Over three centuries ago, Shah Jehan succeeded to the throne of his father Jahangir, and became the third Emperor of India. Although Jehan had many wives, he adored only one. Her name was Mumtaz Mahal, "the Chosen."

They were inseparable. Some say he loved her to distraction, that she was not his wife but his obsession. Victories and riches were as dust compared to her ... in his eyes, she alone was the balm that made life bearable.

When she died Jehan's hair went white. He would break down in tears at the sound of her name. In her memory, he built one of the world's greatest treasures – the Taj Mahal at Agra.

The emperor lived on for many years, but he never forgot his wife. At the last, bedridden, Jehan spent his final days gazing at a reflection of the tomb in a small piece of glass ... still in love with the one they had called "the Chosen."

The glass was found in his hand when he died.

The Food of Love

In the South Pacific, the mango is used in *amrus*, a love potion of considerable potency. Combined with oranges and yogurt, the fruit's invigorating properties make this mousse a delicious aphrodisiac.

Ingredients
Two cups of fresh mango pulp
The finely grated rind of half an orange
Sugar to taste
Half an ounce of gelatine
Two tablespoons of orange juice
Two tablespoons of natural yogurt
Two egg whites

Method
Mix the mango pulp with the rind and sugar. Dissolve the gelatine in the juice and add it and the yogurt to the mango. Leave the mixture until it is almost setting, then whisk the egg whites until stiff and fold them into it. Spoon into glasses and chill until set. A lovely end to a meal and the perfect start to an evening....

A Shepherd's Love

Come live with me and be my Love,
And we will all the pleasures prove
That hills and valleys, dales and fields,
Or woods or steepy mountain yields.

And we will sit upon the rocks,
And see the shepherds feed their flocks
By shallow rivers, to whose falls
Melodious birds sing madrigals.

And I will make thee beds of roses
And a thousand fragrant posies;
A cap of flowers, and a kirtle
Embroidered all with leaves of myrtle.

A gown made of the finest wool
Which from our pretty lambs we pull;
Fair-linèd slippers for the cold,
With buckles of the purest gold.

A belt of straw and ivy-buds
With coral clasps and amber studs:
And if these pleasures may thee move,
Come live with me and be my Love.

The shepherd swains shall dance and sing
For thy delight each May morning:
If these delights thy mind may move,
Then live with me and be my Love.

THE PASSIONATE SHEPHERD TO HIS LOVE
Christopher Marlowe

Cupid and Psyche

Psyche was a mortal princess so beautiful that the Goddess of Love, Venus, was jealous of her and sent her son Cupid to punish her. Yet when Cupid saw Psyche he fell in love with her and had the West Wind carry her to an enchanted place. There each night he wooed her with kind words and denied her nothing, save that which no mortal could be granted: sight of him. Their happiness was almost complete, but Psyche's curiosity was great. One night she lit an oil lamp to behold the one she loved so dearly. Before her was a man of such perfection that the girl was overwhelmed. His beauty filled the room. As she stared, she trembled, and a drop of warm oil fell upon the god's shoulder. He woke and, seeing the lamp, was forced to flee.

Grief-stricken, Psyche wandered in search of her love. Eventually she came to the palace of Venus, who, still jealous of her, set before her fearful tasks that no mortal could ever accomplish. Yet all the forces of Nature combined to aid the sad princess in her adversity and she completed even the most dangerous task – to return from the Regions of the Night with the Box of Beauty. This final test, though, left Psyche exhausted. Fearful lest her lover find her so, she opened the forbidden box to refresh herself. Alas, it contained not Beauty but Death.

Cupid found her in a swoon, the open box by her side. More in love than ever, he vowed that somehow they must be united and begged his father Zeus for pity. The King of Heaven granted his plea, lifted a cup of Ambrosia to Psyche's pale lips and whispered to the princess, "Drink and be immortal, for then you shall truly be the bride of Cupid." Psyche awoke in Cupid's arms and they were never parted again.

A Royal Proposal

"And therefore tell me, most fair Katharine, will you have me? Put off your maiden blushes; avouch the thoughts of your heart with the looks of an empress; take me by the hand, and say 'Harry of England, I am thine:' which word thou shalt no sooner bless mine ear withal, but I will tell thee aloud 'England is thine, Ireland is thine, France is thine, and Henry Plantagenet is thine' … Come, your answer in broken music, – for thy voice is music and thy English broken; therefore, queen of all Katharines, break thy mind to me in broken English, – wilt thou have me?"

HENRY V, ACT 5, SCENE 2
William Shakespeare

Love of Country

Breathes there the man with soul so dead
Who never to himself hath said,
    This is my own, my native land!
Whose heart hath ne'r within him burned,
As home his footsteps he hath turned
        From wandering on a foreign strand ....

BREATHES THERE THE MAN (EXCERPT)
Sir Walter Scott

S*cheherazade*

His Royal Highness Shah Riyár of Samarkand was cruelly disappointed by love. Returning unannounced to his palace one day, he found his queen lying with a slave. Enraged, he slew them both and made a terrible vow: each night he would take a virgin to his bed, but, so he should never be deceived again, she would be put to death at dawn. And it was.

Despair ruled the land until one night an unknown woman came to the palace and asked to lie with the Shah, a woman so beautiful that men sighed when they beheld her. She was called Scheherazade, and when the Shah set his eyes upon her, he felt his heart open.

The night was warm and long and Shah Riyár had never been so charmed by a woman. As the dawn approached, Scheherazade was allowed a last request and she asked to see her sister. A little girl was brought in, whereupon the sisters embraced, holding each other for a long time. The Shah looked away and heard the child beg Scheherazade to tell her a story.

"Most willingly," smiled Scheherazade "if the Shah permits...?"

Shah Riyár, strangely dispirited by the lightening sky, agreed and Scheherazade began her tale. Yet no sooner had the most exciting point been reached than the sun rose and the guards came for the storyteller.

Entranced by the tale, the Shah dismissed them, insisting that Scheherazade return to finish the story the following night. She did so, and so she continued to do for a thousand and one nights, each dawn ending her tale at so enthralling a moment that Shah Riyár would willingly grant her a stay of execution.

Soon it was rumored that His Highness no longer slept at night, desiring no-one's company but Scheherazade's, and, as time passed, it became clear to all that Shah Riyár could never kill this woman who had so completely won his heart. When at last it was heard that he had asked her to become his queen, the whole of Samarkand greeted the dawn with joy.

Acknowledgements

The publishers would like to thank the following for permission to reproduce. ART RESOURCE, NewYork, for *Francesco da Rimini*/Dyce, p. 19; *La Liseuse*/Monet, p. 24; *Faustine*/Arnfield, p. 31; *My Sweet Rose*/Waterhouse, p. 33; *Armore e Psiche*/Gérard, p. 51; *L'Offrande du Coeur*/tapestry, p. 53; *Kneeling Prince*/Islamic miniature, p. 57. THE BRIDGEMAN ART LIBRARY, London, with acknowledgements to: a private collection for *The Year's at the Spring*/Alma-Tadema, p. 16, back flap; Roy Miles Gallery, London, for *The Orchard*/Erichsen, p. 9; Cheltenham Art Gallery and Museums for the 19th c. Valentine, p. 13; the Louvre, Paris, for *The Empress Josephine*/Prud'hon, p. 23; Towneley Hall Art Gallery and Museum, Burnley, for *Destiny*/Waterhouse, p. 29; Österreichische Gallery, Vienna, for *Dinner with Friends*/Engelhard, p. 34; City of Bristol Museum and Art Gallery for *Signing the Register*/Leighton, p. 37; Josef Mensing Gallery, Hamm-Rhynern, for *The Rose Bower*/Zatzka, p. 40-41; Tretyakov Gallery, Moscow, for *The Taj Mahal*/Vereschagin, pp. 44-45; Historiches Museum der Stadt, Vienna, for *The Kiss*/Klimt, p. 47; Manchester City Art Gallery for *The Hireling Shepherd*/Holman Hunt, p. 48; and Gothenburg Art Museum, Sweden, for *Nordic Summer Evening*/Bergh, p. 54. MRS. J. BULL p. 20. FERENS ART GALLERY: HULL CITY MUSEUMS AND ART GALLERIES for *The First Born*/Elwell, pp. 26-27. FINE ART PHOTOGRAPHIC LIBRARY, London, for *The Tempting Prospect*/Trautschold, jacket; *Love at the Stile*/Stone, facing & title page, p. 61; *Betrothed*/Savage, p. 13; *Darby and Joan*, Morgan, p. 15; *Their Youngest Child*/Knight, p. 38. GIRAUDON, Paris, for *La Princesse de Bengale*/Weeks, p. 59. THE BOARD OF TRUSTEES OF THE V. & A. MUSEUM, London, for *Jealousy and Flirtation*/Haynes King, p. 43. WEIDENFELD & NICOLSON for C. Czechowski's translation, first published in *Love Letters* by Antonia Frazer, p. 22. MS. C. M. WHITELAW for the WW1 postcard *Thinking of You*, p. 21.